THE COACH-LIKE LEADER

THE THINGS PEOPLE SAY

Eric Winters is a powerhouse of positive energy, radiating an infectious enthusiasm that leaps off the pages of his latest masterpiece, *The Coach-like Leader*. With a captivating blend of motivational calls to action, profound wisdom, and practical tools that serve as a transformative toolkit, I wholeheartedly endorse Eric's book as the definitive guide for modern leaders seeking to master the art of effective leadership. It's a game-changer!

Jodette Cleary, Chief People & Culture Officer, hipages

As someone who has seen Eric deliver multiple facilitation sessions in person, this book embodies everything he does so well – it's clear, succinct, practical, and holds the essence of what makes a great leader. It's a terrifically useful guide that I know I'll constantly be referring to. I can't recommend this book and Eric's course highly enough to organisations that want their leaders to get to the next level.

Adam Thomas, Organisational Development Specialist, Transport for NSW

Coaching is a must-have skill for 21st century leaders. Eric's companion guide to coaching is an excellent reminder of what is required to be a coach-like leader. It's easy to read, informative and makes the task of understanding coaching a little less complex. I'll be distributing copies to our middle management cohort who attend our leadership development program.

Christopher Simpson, Head of Organisational Learning, Portfolio Agency, Attorney General's Department

Eric's book is refreshingly easy to read, funny and practical but also deeply reflective on the importance of coaching skills for leaders in the 21st century. He has a wonderful way of translating complicated concepts into actionable skills that support and reinforce coaching conversations. He's a natural teacher – his engaging workshops and accessible books combine to deepen this important learning even further.

Claire McCaffery, Head of HR, Accenture Australia and New Zealand

Eric has a wonderful gift of developing your coaching skills in a way that is achievable, builds your confidence and is fun. I've experienced this as part of Eric's facilitation sessions and enjoyed being reminded of how to be a coach-like leader in this book. Being a coach-like leader helps you to create a high-performance environment that values and nurtures the skills and wisdom within every team member. By using the principles within this easy-to-read book, you'll learn how to motivate and support your team members to flourish and succeed.

Gail Bool, Director, Organisational Development, The University of Notre Dame Australia

As someone who understands the importance and impact of coaching in the realm of leadership, I have always believed that effective coaching is the secret sauce behind successful teams. Yet, it's often underutilised.

Enter *The Coach-like Leader* – a gem that not only demystifies the art of coaching but does so in a manner that is incredibly accessible and user-friendly. Every page is packed with invaluable insights, making it a powerful tool for leaders who are always on the go.

If you're a leader who is passionate about fostering a culture of growth, engagement, and inspiration within your team, *The Coach-like Leader* is for you. Don't miss the opportunity to transform your leadership style and, in turn, transform the lives of those you lead.

Natasha Hanney – formerly Culture and Leadership Manager, Westpac

I have been lucky to have experienced Eric Winters as a coaching skills trainer. In *The Coach-like Leader*, Eric has used his vast knowledge of coaching theory to create an easy-to-follow, practical approach to coaching. I believe coaching skills are an essential core competency for any leader – making *The Coach-like Leader* essential reading!

Phoebe Blamey, Director, Clover Financial Solutions

As a lucky recipient of Eric Winters' transformative training in how to coach and develop others, I was excited to learn that he has published *The Coach-like Leader* which contains all of the key concepts that he shared in the training. Easy to read, it's delivered in Eric's usual entertaining and clear style, is a quick reminder of the essential skills needed for the modern coach-like leader that I aspire to be.

The Coach-like Leader will no doubt become an indispensable resource for anyone looking to develop high-performing staff through effective coach-like leadership. I highly recommend Eric's training to all leaders, and this companion guide as a tool for practising the invaluable skills that he teaches.

Anjanette Manwaring, Executive Officer to the Executive Director of IT, Australian Government

Solution-focused conversations to **ignite engagement**, **boost capability** & **launch performance**

ERIC WINTERS

the
COACH-LIKE
LEADER

First published in 2023 by Eric Winters

© Eric Winters 2023
The moral rights of the author have been asserted

A catalogue entry for this book is available from the National Library of Australia.

ISBN: 978-1-923007-62-8

Book production and text design by Publish Central
Cover design by Pipeline Design

The paper this book is printed on is environmentally friendly.

Contents

Introduction

Welcome reader! You're holding *The Coach-like Leader*, the companion guide to a coaching skills training program. You may be discovering these powerful communication skills for the first time or perhaps you're using this book as a refresher. Either way, the coaching skills that follow will transform your leadership forever. Buckle up.

You're going to become a more coach-like leader who:

- improves employee performance now and develops their capability for the future
- has empowering conversations that improve working relationships
- encourages team members to take ownership, build responsibility and develop accountability
- enables high-performing teams to get better at independently solving problems
- promotes your own career growth with a critical leadership capability.

It would be awesome if we could develop coaching skills just by reading about them (or better yet, downloading them effortlessly into our brains, Matrix style). Can't be done. We learn by doing. So, this little book isn't a substitute for training – it's supplemental. It's a pool of ideas you'll cover in your training. These pages are somewhere to dive into for reimmersion and concept refreshment.

I'm optimistic you'll find this is an easy read, something you'll happily pick up. I'm aiming for light-hearted and practical. Less superfluous packaging and bubble-wrap, more useful content.

Two things

A few words about effort and competency. You'll get more out of the training if you're willing to do two things. Thing one: to apply the skills taught. Thing two: to suck. Initially. Competence lies on the other side of incompetence. There are no detours around or tunnels beneath. You've got to wade through. It's going to be messy at times.

Over the last ten years I've trained over a thousand leaders and professional coaches to learn coaching skills in programs like the one you're doing. Time and again participants tell me they are amazed to discover the power of coaching conversations. But only when they're willing to do Thing one and Thing two. Repeatedly.

So be kind to yourself as you learn these skills. You're supposed to be clunky for a while.

You've embarked on a coaching skills course for leaders and managers. You won't be learning how to be a professional coach but you will be developing skills to be a more coach-like leader. You'll discover you can have coaching conversations with anyone; your teams (individually or together), peers, your own leadership, suppliers, friends, partners and even yourself. For the sake of convenience, I'll refer to the person you're coaching as 'the team member' or 'the coachee', and I'll refer to the person doing the coaching as 'the coach-like leader' or 'the coach'.

The best way to use this book is to dip in as needed *after* the workshops. It's a refresher remember, not a replacement.

A sneak peek

Let's take a sneak peek at what's inside.

In chapter one you'll meet the coach-like leader. We'll explore what coaching really is and make a case for considering it a critical leadership capability.

In chapter two you'll discover the three conditions for effective coaching. When even one is absent, conversations will be effortful and unproductive. You don't want that.

Coaching is a very versatile conversational skill – you'll quickly find it's highly relevant to many workplace interactions. Chapter three presents seven situations in which being more coach-like can help. (It's also relevant to interactions outside work, but that's not our focus.) You'll quickly discover that solution-focused conversations like this are going to be really helpful in professional *and* personal life.

Coaching is characterised by a particular set of core conversational ingredients – use them in the right amounts and at the right times and you'll catalyse others' thinking ability. Chapter four identifies these ingredients – the behaviours and skills that constitute effective coaching.

One critical conversational skill in particular – listening – gets chapter five all to itself. You'll discover how listening like an alpaca builds respect, rapport and performance. You'll never think of active listening in quite the same way again.

To keep your coaching conversations on track, in chapter six we'll unpack the most popular coaching framework of all time: GROW. Much of coaching involves helping others think new thoughts. To achieve this, you'll need some powerful questions. I'll provide a starter set you can use throughout the GROW framework.

Much of human communication isn't what we say, it's *how*. We're always communicating with our bodies, gestures, expressions, tone and emphasis. If we want our coachees to experience our coaching presence as truly enabling, we'll need to employ all these skilfully. This is covered in chapter seven. Since we're spending considerable time communicating online now, we'll also look at how to elevate online conversations.

Coaching conversations are also a skilful means of amplifying motivation and engagement. We'll look at the key principles you'll need to know to do this well in chapter eight.

Finally, we'll look at common coaching challenges. Chapter nine discusses how leaders sometimes inadvertently undermine their coaching effectiveness, and what to do about it.

Learning coaching skills is an exciting journey. I'm confident you're going to hugely enjoy your training, and deeply value the advantages learning these skills will give you throughout your working life.

Let's dive in!

Eric

1: Meet the Coach-like Leader

"It takes **courage to ask a question** rather than offer up advice, provide an answer or unleash a solution."

Brené Brown

ob Dylan released *The Times They Are a-Changin'* in 1964. They were, and they haven't stopped. Change has impacted every aspect of living and working since. Old ways of managing and leading are increasingly irrelevant to meeting today's workplace challenges.

Our 21st century workplaces have been reshaped by changes in technology, globalisation, competition and evolving cultural expectations. Many of us now work from home, with colleagues distributed geographically. As the world's workforce is increasingly well educated and tech-savvy, competition has expanded. It's not only local, it's international, bold and ambitious. Pressures to curb costs demand that leaders do more with less. Public sector organisations are also under continual pressure to demonstrate greater value for money.

Today's professionals have different expectations too. They don't just want any job, they want a *great* job. Social media stokes ambitions. Millennials and Generation Z don't just want a paycheque and promotion, they want purpose and development. They expect respect, meaningful work, personal and professional growth, and fulfillment. In short, they want to be engaged at work.

The value of engaged workers

This is fortunate, because more than ever, organisations need engaged workers. Business consultancy Gallup reports that worker engagement is strongly connected to workplace results. Engaged workers have:

- 41% less absenteeism

- 70% fewer safety incidents

- 59% lower turnover

- 10% higher customer satisfaction metrics

- 17% higher productivity.

That's not all. Engaged workers are more collaborative, adaptable and resilient, more innovative, do higher quality work, enjoy better health and wellbeing, and improve their organisation's reputation to help attract top talent and increase profitability.

What's not to like?

Unfortunately, in Australia only 20% of workers are engaged (that is, involved, enthusiastic and committed to the organisational mission). The rest include 'quiet quitters' and the actively hostile.

So, what's the biggest contributor to employee engagement? Well, it's not gym membership, office bean bags or lunchtime yoga. It turns out 70% of engagement is due to the manager or leader. How people lead has a wildly disproportionate impact on how people experience their working life. It's said that people don't leave jobs, they leave managers. You don't want to be that manager.

The different leadership styles

Leadership thought leader Daniel Goleman identified six distinct leadership styles in his book *Leadership That Gets Results*.[1] The most effective leaders use these styles flexibly depending on the circumstances. The least used of these styles – and the one with the greatest potential to improve engagement – is the Coaching leadership style.

Coach-like leaders focus on the development of their team members. They enable performance by communicating in ways that empower others. They provide guidance, support and feedback to help others improve skills and realise more of their potential. This style is effective for long-term employee development and growth.

---

1   These are: Coercive leaders, Authoritative leaders, Affiliative leaders, Democratic leaders, Pacesetting leaders and Coaching leaders.

Less effective leaders may overplay one of the other leadership styles, such as Coercive leadership. This style is characterised by a top-down authoritarian approach. Leaders who use this style demand immediate compliance and expect their orders to be followed without question. To be sure, being directive still has its place. When someone is inexperienced, when time is short or when processes must be followed, providing clear and comprehensive direction may be the best way to go.

But when this style is overplayed, it promotes passive obedience over proactive productivity. Employees' current intelligence and future potential remained untapped.

This kind of leader is more of a boss than a coach.

As Gallup say in the *Wall Street Journal* #1 bestseller *It's the Manager*, today's workers don't want a boss, they want a coach. They want a coach-like leader who asks more and tells less.

Today's workers don't want a boss, they want a coach-like leader who **asks more and tells less**.

FROM BOSS

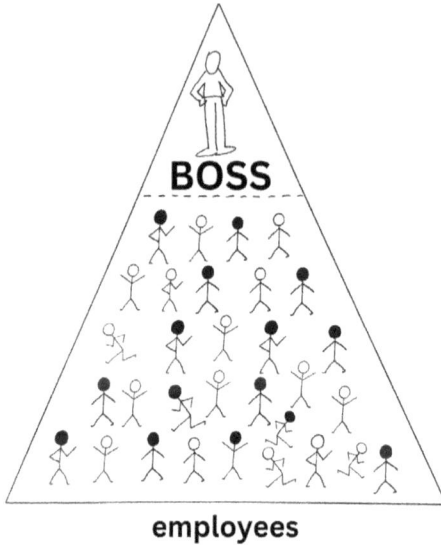

BOSS

employees

Characteristics of bossing

Distant relationships
Telling others what to do
Micromanagement
Neglect
Annual feedback
Deciding how to manage staff
Training for today

TO COACH

employees

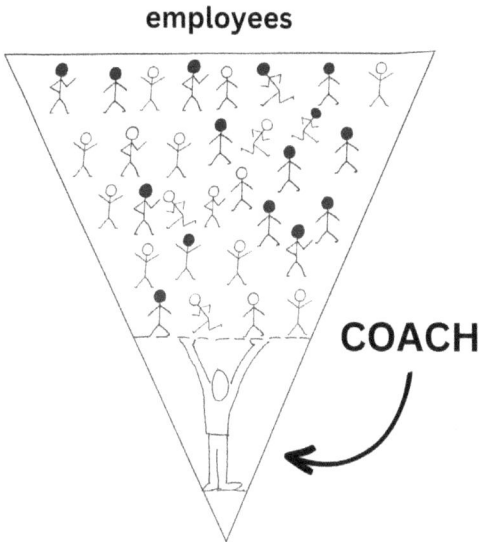

COACH

Characteristics of coaching

Close relationships
Collaborative goal setting
Trust
Frequent check-ins
Ongoing feedback
Asking staff how they are best managed
Development for career growth

So, what does coaching look like at work?

Coaching is a collaborative, solution-focused conversation. It's a conversation to help someone think, learn and plan. Then take action. It's a very empowering way to talk to someone. It's respectful and encouraging. It demonstrates trust. People generally like being spoken to this way. They do much better work and enjoy the growth that follows. They take on feedback more willingly. They're more engaged at work and committed to the organisation they work for.

The ability to coach others is a core leadership capability in the 21st century. Coaching others is how effective leaders access current capability and develop potential.

In the coaching course you're taking you'll learn how and when to have coaching conversations. You'll learn how to speak and listen to others in a way that amplifies their creativity and ownership. You'll build rapport and trust. You'll develop capability and get better results.

You'll be able to apply this style of communicating to team members, diverse stakeholders and even to yourself – after all, you probably talk to yourself more than to anyone else. Why not make those conversations more productive too?

Coaching is a collaborative, solution-focused conversation to help someone think, learn and plan. **And take action.**

2: Conditions for Coaching

Coach-like leaders create the conditions for **courageous thinking and high performance**.

always liked the idea of having a kitchen garden – somewhere I could grow my own herbs and vegetables. So, when I moved home, I was thrilled to have a small courtyard with an empty garden bed. It was time to get growing. I could see myself garnishing homemade curries with home-grown coriander in no time. I planted and waited. And waited.

To my immense surprise and disappointment, nothing much grew except weeds, and even they didn't appear to have their heart in it. A green-fingered friend diagnosed the problem. Not enough light, awful soil and excessive watering. The conditions were all wrong.

When we're helping others to think, learn and grow through coaching conversations, we need to get the conditions right. When we do, employees will be more creative. They'll learn better and take greater ownership. They'll thrive and develop. Get the conditions wrong and, just like my garden, nothing useful will grow.

Nurturing high performance

It's not your role to nourish team members with food and water but it *is* your responsibility to create the conditions for courageous thinking and the high performance that follow. There are three critical ingredients for this to occur.

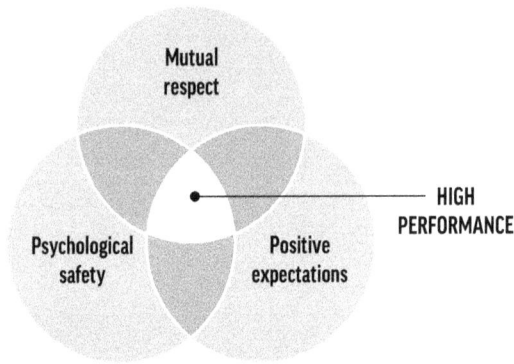

Mutual respect

When you think of social creatures, maybe bees, ants or meerkats come to mind. The most social species on earth, however, is humans. We collaborate like no other animal or bug ever will. Our ancestors stayed alive through effective teamwork. They hunted for food in groups, they defended themselves from predators and hostile tribes in groups. There's safety within a friendly tribe. However, if the tribe didn't value you or your contributions, you were out.

Instead of being at the top of the food chain, you became a link further down. Perhaps you became big cat food.

So good relationships matter. When someone treats us respectfully, it tells us we matter to them. The experience of feeling respected is essential for full-throttle collaboration. In another chapter I'll share how important it is that we're non-judgemental when we're coaching someone. I'll confess in advance; that's a half-truth. No one wants to be negatively judged, but everyone wants to be positively evaluated. To be valued. When we demonstrate respect, we're showing someone they matter to us. We care about them. The experience of being respected activates a collaborative 'we' mindset rather than a defensive 'me' mindset. It's essential for effective coaching.

It's not enough that you respect your coachees, they need to respect you too. Help them to respect you by being the kind of person worthy of their respect. We'll discuss building trust shortly.

Coach-like leaders show respect to team members in many ways, such as:

- valuing contributions
- expressing appreciation
- empowering others to make decisions
- respecting work–life balance
- ensuring fairness and equity
- celebrating diversity and inclusion

- believing in others' current capability and future potential.

A final word on respect. It's not enough that the coach-like leader respects their teams. What matters is that team members *experience* that respect. They need to see it, hear it, feel it. It's the experience of being respected that is necessary for effective coaching. Coach-like leaders show it.

Positive expectations

We all perform better when we face a challenge. It's how we grow muscles and how we grow skills and careers. Coach-like leaders have high expectations of the capability and potential of their people to do great work. They challenge team members to step up, confident that they can do so when supported. They believe in their people and hold them accountable for meeting their positive expectations.

Accountability is the responsibility of individuals to answer for their actions, decisions and the consequences of their behaviour. It encompasses transparency, integrity and the willingness to accept the consequences of actions, whether positive or negative. It often involves setting clear expectations, tracking performance and holding individuals responsible for achieving their commitments.

We all raise our game when we're held accountable. A professional doesn't like letting others, or themselves, down. We want to be seen as reliable and dependable. As someone who means what we say.

The coach-like leader holds team members accountable. After all, they have high expectations of their people. It's a curious thing that humans have a habit of meeting the expectations of others. Whether you expect a lot of people or a little, they'll often prove you right.

Psychological safety

Organisational psychologist and bestselling author Adam Grant describes psychological safety as 'a climate of respect, trust, and openness in which people can raise concerns and suggestions without fear of reprisal'.[2] He identifies psychological safety as the foundation of all learning cultures.

When we don't feel at risk of being criticised, evaluated or punished, we're more willing to:

· be honest
· share our tentative ideas
· admit mistakes
· ask for help
· receive and act on feedback
· voice ambitions
· express concerns
· think boldly
· try something new.

---

2   *Think Again: The power of knowing what you don't know* by Adam Grant.

The experience of psychological safety is essential to nourish coaching conversations. So how is it developed? We feel safe with those we trust. When we build trust, we build safety.

Building trust

What kind of people do you trust most in your working life? Trust is an expectation that people will behave in a certain way. We're trusting that they'll have certain characteristics. Here are some important ones.

Authentic
vulnerable and real

Accountable
apologises when
they fall short

Confidentiality
personal info
stays personal

Competence
know what
they're doing

Credit
given where it's due

Consistency
reliable and
dependable

Helpful
they have your back

Honest
tell it like it is

Care
has your best
interests at heart

TRUST

Let's take a look at each of these.

Authentic

We trust people we experience as real. They're not hiding behind a mask, they really mean what they say and live in a way that's aligned with their values. As a result, they're credible. What you see is what you get. Authentic people are willing, at times, to be vulnerable. They'll admit mistakes and errors of judgment, and voice concerns. Authentic people are willing to share something of their own lives, hopes and ambitions. We feel like we know them.

Confidentiality

We trust those who can keep a secret. We know any sensitive information we may share will go no further. As a result, it's safe to be open and honest.

Credit

We trust leaders who assign credit where it's due. They don't use our wins to bolster themselves, rather they'll ensure our successful efforts are recognised as our own. They're in our corner. They advocate on our behalf.

Helpful

We trust our allies. Those who want to assist, enable and empower us. Those who facilitate our progress. Coaching conversations are all about helping others do great work and develop their capabilities.

Care

We trust those we experience as having our best interests at heart. They're committed to supporting our professional development and growth. They look out for opportunities for us to learn, build skills and be helpfully challenged. They know and care about our ambitions, our lives in and out of work, our wellbeing. We matter to them. Effective leaders demonstrate that they care through their interactions.

Honest

We trust people who are honest with us. We trust that they'll share information we need to know, when possible. We trust they'll let us know swiftly when we're off course. Honest people are transparent. They're frank and willing to say the things that others might withhold.

Consistency

We trust those who are reliable and dependable. They do what they said they would. Their mood is stable rather than erratic. They're the same person this week as they were last week. Consistency fuels certainty, which builds trust.

Competence

We trust people who know what they're doing. They've got a track record of excellence in a particular field. We can depend on them for their expertise. Paradoxically, we also trust people who are willing to say when they don't have expertise or don't have an answer. They're all the more credible for revealing their knowledge and skills gaps. They don't pretend to know it all. Phoneys have a certain scent. It's unpleasant and erodes trust.

Accountable

We trust people who hold themselves accountable. They take ownership for their commitments and hold themselves responsible rather than making excuses. In the event they drop the ball, they apologise and make amends. Apologising is a demonstration of emotional intelligence. Contrast this with the fragile, fearful leader who can never admit they made a mistake. Could you ever really trust someone like that?

Trust must be earned

Trust is something that's earned. It's developed over time through demonstrations of being trustworthy. Being honest. Being accountable. Being authentic. Building trust is a little like putting coins in a jar. You make small deposits which build over time.

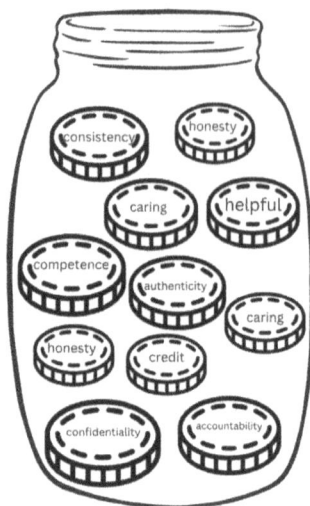

Of course, if you drop a jar, it will break in an instant. Trust can also be broken quickly through violations of the contract of trust. Effective coach-like leaders are quick to apologise for such violations. Demonstrations of accountability like this can even make trust stronger than before.

"Trust is the glue of life. **It's the most essential ingredient** in effective communication. It's the foundational principle that holds all relationships."

Stephen R. Covey

3: Seven Coaching Conversations

"Leadership is not about being in charge. It is about **taking care of those in your charge**."

Simon Sinek

Coaching conversations will be helpful any time you want someone to take ownership, learn from experience, improve performance or develop their talent. Coaching conversations also build engagement in others, improve working relationships and liberate you to do more of your own work.

When might a coach-like leader want to enable others in this way?

Funny you should ask. Here are seven suggestions:

1. goal-setting conversations

2. feedback conversations

3. learning conversations

4. planning conversations

5. developmental conversations

6. problem-solving conversations

7. check-in conversations.

Let's take a look at each of these.

1. Goal-setting conversations

People like, as far as possible, to choose their own direction. They are more motivated to pursue goals they've co-created, rather than ones they've been given. To be self-directed.

Goals take many forms – in addition to meeting team targets they can include developing industry or technical expertise, cultivating relationship skills, broadening networks and other professional developmental goals.

According to a leading model of human motivation, Self-Determination Theory, people have three core needs.[3] When they're all met, we're engaged, motivated and feel empowered to do our best work. When one or more are unmet, we're more likely to be disillusioned, dispirited and watching the clock.

The three core needs are:

1. **Autonomy:** to be self-directed, to choose our own way.

2. **Competence:** to feel up to the task at hand, and that we're getting better.

3. **Relatedness:** to feel like we're among allies, and we're supported, valued and trusted.

Experiencing each one matters, but the sense of autonomy is the most important.

---

3   *Self-Determination Theory: Basic psychological needs in motivation, development, and wellness* by Richard M. Ryan and Edward L. Deci.

The coach-like leader helps their team experience autonomy through collaborative goal setting, to whatever extent possible. As a consequence, members feel like they are piloting their careers in personally meaningful directions rather than being passengers on someone else's journey.

Of course, leaders don't always have the liberty to let others choose their own goals. After all, your team has specific objectives to meet. But the more choice you can provide in *how* your people will achieve their targets, the more engagement they'll experience. Effective coach-like leaders help their people to experience whatever autonomy is available.

2. Feedback conversations

Professionals like to know how they're doing. They want to know when they're on track, and they need to know when they're off track. Millennials and Generation Z in particular expect frequent feedback. However, few know how to deliver feedback effectively. Coaching can help.

Providing constructive feedback

At some point in our careers, most of us have received critical feedback delivered clumsily. It's not pleasant.

It's little wonder this happens – most leaders and managers have been given no training in skilfully providing constructive feedback. As a result, leaders dread having the conversation with staff, delay it, and finally let them have it! They'll take a directive and possibly adversarial stance, declaring what was done wrong and what had *better be done correctly next time*. It's less a conversation and more of a critical monologue.

When feedback is delivered this way, people feel attacked. Inevitably, they'll be defensive. They'll be resistant to hearing and accepting the message and less willing to change their behaviour. The result is offended workers, damaged relationships and disengagement. It's miserable for everyone concerned.

But the coach-like leader knows how to handle these situations.

They'll take a curious and collaborative stance. They'll have a conversation swiftly after poor performance – not letting frustration build up – and will want to hear the coachee's perspective. How do they think they're doing? What were their intentions when they did such and such? What were they hoping to achieve? What's their assessment of how it went?

After listening to the coachee they'll share their own observations. What they've noticed the coachee has done and what the consequences were. The conversation is about modifiable coachee behaviours, not immutable coachee personality flaws.

They'll then have a collaborative conversation around how they might move forward. What do they need to do better? How might they go about that? What will they try first?

Coachees leave such feedback sessions feeling supported, valued and trusted. Relationships are stronger and engagement is higher.

Providing positive feedback

Many leaders underappreciate the power of letting others know when they're doing well. You'll recall (you do remember this, don't you?) one of the three conditions of coaching is genuine respect. To respect someone is to value them. Effective leaders let their teams know they value them by saying so.

Like constructive feedback, positive feedback can be done poorly or well. Simply telling someone 'great job' or 'you're the best' will provide a quick flush of wellbeing, but it's not very helpful. What *specifically* is it you appreciate and why? What would you like them to repeat?

Effective positive feedback is also given swiftly, and it identifies the action taken and the positive impact it had. It also expresses appreciation for skills, strengths and effort. Just like the constructive feedback, you're focusing on behaviours, on what's within the coachee's control.

Being given appreciative feedback is highly motivating in three ways. Firstly, people feel their efforts are being noticed. Secondly, they feel their efforts are valued by you. This improves your relationship. Thirdly, they experience personal competency.

You'll recall good relationships and competency were two of the three human needs. Experiencing these is critical to engagement and job satisfaction.

Expect people to do more of what you thank them for.

3. Learning conversations

There's opportunity for a learning conversation after any event or series of events at work. After a project, a presentation, a problem, a meeting – anything. Whatever has happened, the coach-like leader can facilitate a learning conversation afterwards. This is worthwhile if the event went well or not. There's always something to learn.

The best time to conduct these reviews is immediately afterwards while memories are fresh – do not wait for an annual performance review, although that is also an opportunity to consolidate learning.

The coach-like leader facilitates a collaborative learning conversation by first exploring what went well. Acknowledging successes first puts people into a more resilient and receptive headspace, which will be needed to fully take ownership of errors, mistakes and mishaps.

Questions can include:

- What went well?
- What contributed to that success?
- What positive impact did that have?

- How did that impact the results?
- What would you choose to do again?

After unpacking the successes, the coach-like leader can help others acknowledge and learn from what didn't go so well. We might ask:

- What would you do differently next time?
- What was missing?
- What was the impact?
- What did you do that was less helpful?
- What didn't you do that, in hindsight, would have been worthwhile?

Coaching conversations of this sort are opportunities for honest appraisal, review and improvement. Done well, people feel supported and valued, and they develop their capability. In organisations with coaching cultures, people look forward to reviews. They're opportunities to work better together now, and in the future.

4. Planning conversations

Any time you want an upcoming event to go well, you could just hope for the best. That might work. Alternatively, you could be more intentional and have planning conversations.

Of course, people can plan by themselves. But we all think better when we're in the presence of people who are supportive, interested and willing to do two things:

· ask questions we might not have thought of ourselves

· listen to the answers.

When we think out loud with a coach-like leader we come up with more options, see obstacles we hadn't considered and generate more solutions. As a result, we're more likely to make better decisions.

In *The Seven Habits of Highly Effective People*, author Stephen Covey encourages us to **begin with the end in mind**.[4] Accordingly, coach-like leaders help others really consider what success looks like. They might ask:

· If this goes really well, what will happen?

· What will that look like?

· What would you notice?

· What will people be saying?

· What difference will that make?

· What's important about those differences?

---

4   Habit 1: Be proactive, Habit 2: Begin with the end in mind, Habit 3: Put first things first, Habit 4: Think win–win, Habit 5: Seek first to understand, then to be understood, Habit 6: Synergise, Habit 7: Sharpen the saw.

Behavioural psychologist Gabriele Oettingen encourages people to plan using a four-step framework she calls WOOP:[5]

W this is the Wish. What is it you really want to have happen?

O the Outcome. What would you experience if you achieve your wish? What would that be like?

O Obstacles. What might get in the way?

P Plan. What do you need to do to realise your wish, experience the outcome and manage the obstacles?

We'll talk more about motivation in chapter 8. In the meantime, know that people aren't motivated by facts, they're motivated by feelings. What generates motivational feelings is anticipating needs and desires being met, and threats being avoided. In a planning conversation we want to help coachees articulate their WOOP.

---

5   *Rethinking Positive Thinking: Inside the new science of motivation* by Gabriele Oettingen.

5. Developmental conversations

Millennials and Generation Z have an appetite for purposeful growth. They want careers in which their individual development is supported, encouraged and nourished. They'll leave organisations where they stagnate, and invest themselves wholeheartedly in workplaces that invest in them.

The coach-like leader takes time to understand the strengths and aspirations of their people. They ask them about work experiences that have been rewarding in the past, and have exploratory conversations about what a fulfilling career might look like in the future. They appreciate where their coachees have been and are allies in helping them get to where they want to go.

In these collaborative conversations the coach-like leader helps the coachee construct a personally meaningful developmental path. Together they'll identify targets for technical and personal developmental growth. Together they'll build plans for skills training and exposure to developmental opportunities. It's up to the coachee to enact the plans – this is their career, they own it. The coach-like leader reviews the coachee's progress and assists them in making adjustments.

Developmental conversations should happen at least twice a year. Any less and staff are more likely to experience this as an insincere tick-and-flick exercise.

6. Problem-solving conversations

Directive leaders have a habit of solving other people's problems for them. *Got a problem? Here's what you should do. Let me show you.*

They mean well. They may do this to save time, to make life easier for others, to teach or to demonstrate their expertise. Paradoxically, 'helping' others by taking away their problems can sometimes disempower them. They learn dependency. They fail to learn to take ownership and fail to develop problem-solving skills of their own. Any sense of competency becomes fragile.

Coach-like leaders support staff to think through their own problems and resolve them for themselves.

As expressed earlier, we all think better when we articulate our thoughts in the presence of someone who is interested, supportive and believes in us.

Perhaps you've experienced this firsthand. You had a problem at work, you called someone over to talk about it and then BANG, the solution popped into your head as you talked it through. Some of my workshop participants tell me they've solved their own problems as someone else approached *before* they'd said a word out loud.

In coaching conversations, we want to understand the problem and then steer the conversation towards a solution. It's the responsibility of the coach-like leader to keep the conversation solution-focused.

We might ask questions such as:

- What's the problem specifically?
- When does the problem occur?
- When doesn't the problem occur?
- What makes the difference?
- What factors are contributing to this situation?
- What have you tried so far to resolve it?
- What would you like to have happen?
- What might help?
- What difference might that make?
- What needs to happen?
- How will you know when the problem is resolved?

Coachees who are supported in this way develop their own problem-solving skills, boost their confidence and dial up their sense of competence. They'll come to you less and less.

7. Check-in conversations

Coaching conversations needn't be formal, scheduled, lengthy events – they can be brief, informal and ad-hoc. A good example of this is the check-in conversation.

Millennials and Generation Z want ongoing conversations with their leaders – they want to feel like they and their roles matter. When the coach-like leader checks in, they're showing interest in their people's progress, holding them accountable and offering support.

The frequency of the check-in lies on a continuum, with micromanagement at one end and neglectful lack of interest at the other. The sweet spot will shift depending on the coachee's experience and competence regarding the task at hand. These ongoing conversations could happen once a day or twice a week.

Check-ins are friendly and supportive inquiries. The tone of the questions is key: you're asking because you're interested, not because you don't trust them. Body language matters here (we'll say more about this in chapter 7). For now, know that reports are generally highly sensitive to their leaders' behaviours. They're constantly unconsciously asking themselves, 'Does my leader like me? Value me? Trust me?' Show them you do.

Check-in conversations can include questions such as:

- How are you getting along with X?
- Where are at with Y?
- How did Z go?
- What have you learned?
- What might you do again?
- Why might you do differently next time?
- What's the real objective?

- How will you prepare for that?
- What might get in the way?
- How might you prepare for that?
- What's the next step?

Hopefully some of these questions are seeming familiar by now. Coaching conversations follow similar principles; it's just the situation that's different.

* * *

We've just taken a look at seven coaching conversations. You've seen how this solution-focused style of communication is such a highly versatile approach to boosting performance now and building capability for the future. These conversations provide helpful approaches to learning from the past, resolving challenges in the present and boosting performance and skills in the future.

"We rise **by lifting others**."

Robert Ingersoll

4: Coaching Behaviours and Skills

"The power
of coaching is
**in the questions
you ask**, not
the answers
you provide."

Michael Bungay Stanier

The seven coaching conversations introduced in the previous chapter may have different objectives, but they're united by common characteristics. Let's take a look at what differentiates coaching from other ways of interacting with people.

Coaching conversations are helpfully unbalanced

In much of life, when two people are having a 'good' conversation there's probably a certain amount of balance. Both get roughly equal airtime. We talk a bit about you. We talk a bit about me. We listen to each other. It's balanced.

Coaching conversations are unbalanced in very specific ways. This is what makes them so powerful. In this chapter we'll look at the unbalanced characteristics of coaching conversations. We'll examine the behaviours and skills that coach-like leaders use to develop their people.

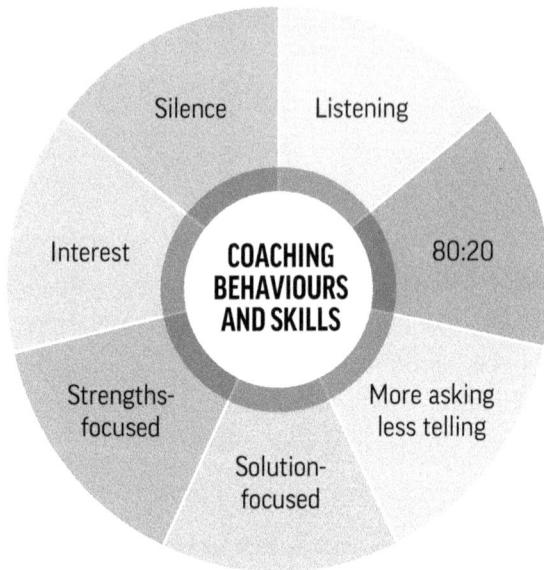

More asking less telling

Coach-like leaders are slow to give advice. They're skilled at asking questions that help others to think things through for themselves. They ask a lot of questions.

Not telling others what to do may be the biggest challenge for leaders developing their coaching skills. You probably do know best. Wouldn't it save a lot of time and get a better result if you just told them what they ought to do and how to do it?

Well, yes, in the short term, it would. However, we get better by being challenged. By thinking for ourselves.

If we think for other people, we run the risk of debilitating instead of developing them.

Coaching someone now is an investment. Tasks may take longer in the short term, but by developing your people you'll have less to do in the longer term.

Solution-focused

Q: How long can people talk about their problems?
A: For as long as you'll let them.

There's something painfully delicious about harping on about our woes, losses, setbacks and disappointments. We love to talk about what's missing, unfair, broken or wrong. But soaking in the satisfyingly steamy waters of negativity doesn't make things better. In fact, it saps our energy to do anything to make things better. It's disempowering.

The coach-like leader will acknowledge problems and challenges, but after that they steer the conversation towards generating solutions. The coach keeps the conversation oriented towards what we want, why it matters and how we'll get there. This is empowering.

The coach has a responsibility to keep the conversation on track. I'll provide a framework for doing this later, but for now, know that the role of the coach is to keep the conversation solution-focused; that is, on what is wanted.

Strengths-focused

Strengths are anything people are good at and that energise them when they do it. It's often a quality that comes naturally to them. People often take their strengths for granted, assuming perhaps that everyone can do what they can. Nope.

Some examples of strengths might include being strategic, explaining things clearly, problem-solving, building rapport, being humorous and optimising time.

Anything we focus on is amplified in our awareness. Coach-like leaders energise their team members by focusing on their strengths and team members energise themselves when they use their strengths.

Coach-like leaders recognise their employees' strengths, name them, and help others to own them and apply them. When people feel capable, they think better and are proactive. It's empowering.

Coach-like leaders know their people. Over time, they learn what talents and capabilities they already possess. They know what energises them. Discovering the strengths of others can emerge through conversations and experience, but many organisations choose to accelerate strength identification with an online strength assessment tool such as the Gallup CliftonStrengths or the Cappfinity Strengths Profile. We'll say more about this in chapter 8.

80:20 airtime

Coaches are generous conversationalists. They give coachees space to think and speak. They're patient. They listen. They're quiet.

This means in a coaching conversation the coachee does most of the talking. This could be as much as 80% to 90% of the time. Extroverts in particular find conversational restraint very taxing. For talkative people, it can be very difficult not to say more.

So, there's a significant imbalance in who is doing most of the speaking. More than that, when the coach-like leader does speak, their contributions are short. Coaches speak in sentences, the coached speak in paragraphs.

Silence

Coach-like leaders are good at *not* talking. They are mostly silent at three different times.

Firstly, they do not speak after asking a question. Even if the coachee is quiet. If the coachee is quiet, they don't jump in and fill the space with their noise. They remain silent. This generous silence gives the coachee room to think without feeling rushed.

Secondly, they tend not to interrupt others while they are speaking. This would derail their thinking. Of course, we're not going to be completely silent when someone is talking to us. We'll want to demonstrate we're paying attention and be supportive with sounds of encouragement: 'Oh.' 'Uh huh.' 'Right.' 'I see.' 'Mmmm.'

Thirdly, they're quiet for a moment after the coachee has finished speaking. Maybe they haven't finished after all – maybe more ideas will emerge if they're just given a little space.

Be interested

Have you ever had a conversation with someone who wasn't really interested in what you had to say? Of course you have! Maybe they kept checking their phone or their eyes gave away that their attention had wandered. Not very pleasant, is it?

It's hard to continue a conversation when the person you're speaking to isn't engaged or is just going through the motions – why bother? On the other hand, when we're with someone who's really interested it's much easier to think and talk. Ideas flow.

Everyone thinks more effectively in the presence of an interested listener. When someone else cares about what we say, we think better. It's like getting a brain upgrade.

Coach-like leaders are interested in what others think. They demonstrate that interest through their engagement, their body language, their tonality, their questions.

Be non-judgemental

We think best in the presence of people who accept and value us just as we are and believe we are capable of more. But when we're in the presence of critics, we feel guarded and vulnerable. It shuts us down.

A good coach avoids giving the coachee the experience of being negatively judged, evaluated or criticised. They receive a coachee's ideas with curiosity and interest. Even if they disagree, they'll withhold swift dismissal of their coachee's thinking, asking instead for clarification. They help coachees feel supported and valued. As a result, the coachees think more effectively and are more open to feedback, acknowledging mistakes and being held accountable.

This doesn't mean that coach-like leaders never disagree with their coachees. They'll certainly voice any concerns. But it's done with kindness, sensitivity and tact. All ideas are welcome, even the less helpful ones. Fail to do this and coachees will avoid sharing their thinking in future.

Be a great listener

Coach-like leaders are great listeners. And not only do they listen, but coachees have the experience of being listened to. It's this experience that catalyses thinking.

Most people can't listen well. The best they can do is wait to speak. And they may not even be able to do that, butting in to steer the conversation back to themselves and what they think.

This topic deserves a bit more space. It deserves a whole chapter. I've given it one.

5: ALPACA Listening

"**Listening is an art** that requires attention over talent, spirit over ego, others over self."

Dean Jackson

Did you know alpacas have excellent hearing? It's true – not only are they great listeners they also have implausibly sweet faces. There's a lot to love about them. But we'll concentrate on the listening bit.

It turns out that listening well is one of the core ingredients to high-performance coaching, and it can be done well without large furry adjustable ears.

Great work emerges from great relationships, great relationships develop through great conversations and great conversations are built on great listening. It's the foundation of high-performance teams.

How many people do you know though who consistently listen *really* well? Not just hearing what you're saying but giving you all their attention and being fully present? People who give you the experience of being deeply heard and understood? Who make you feel like you and your thinking *really* matter?

In my experience, they're rare. They stand out as exceptional leaders. When they listen, they listen actively.

Active listening consists of a combination of skills. Listening this way builds rapport, respect and a sense of safety, it catalyses thinking and encourages speaking, exploration and discovery. When we listen to others this way, it's like giving them a brain upgrade. As a result, people perform better.

In the presence of an active listener, team members:

· think better out loud

· solve problems sooner

· see more possibilities

· take ownership for their mistakes

· take responsibility for their choices

· are more creative

· are more proactive

· develop self-confidence

· learn from successes and setbacks

· are more ambitious

· make plans and take action.

Active listening is a foundational skill for great leadership and optimal working relationships.

So, what does an active listener actually do?

A ASKING A QUESTION

L LISTENING TO THE ANSWER

P PAUSING BEFORE RESPONDING

A ACKNOWLEDGING WHAT WE HEARD

C CHECKING OUR UNDERSTANDING

A ASKING ANOTHER QUESTION

A framework for active listening

When we're active listening, we're doing six things.

A Asking a question

L Listening to the answer

P Pausing before responding

A Acknowledging what we heard

C Checking our understanding

A Asking another question

When we do each of these well, the person we're actively listening to will have an empowering experience. And that's the point of coaching: to empower others to think, learn, plan and act more effectively.

Let's take a look at each step.

Ask a question

We want to ask questions that help people think more effectively. Empowering questions. The kind of questions that will do this are lonely, brief and open.

A **lonely question** is one you send in all by itself. One question at a time. You don't bunch up your questions into a confusing hot mess. That's called 'drive-by questioning'. It's an act of conversational violence. Just ask a single question. That way the receiver doesn't need to track all your questions and decide which one to answer first. That would be hard work. Hard work's good, but not yet. Confusing people unnecessarily now would waste the cognitive energy they'll need later for planning.

A **brief question** has few words. It's easy to understand. Brevity is clarity. Again, we're trying to avoid wasting energy and losing thinking momentum. So, keep your questions as short as possible.

Open questions invite exploration and elaboration. They often begin with 'how' or 'what'.

What leads you to that conclusion?

What is the significance of that?

How would your proposal impact … ?

You'll recall that closed questions can be answered by a word or two. They have their place, but often we want to encourage others to expand their thinking. It's through articulating partially formed thoughts that people discover more of what they already think and develop their thinking further. We want to help people say more and think further.

I'm tempted to jump ahead to the L in ALPACA. But there's something else that's important about asking great questions. It's not just about what you say. It's *how*. How we ask a question makes all the difference.

When someone asks you a question with genuine curiosity, it fuels your thinking. If someone asks you a question in an indifferent way, well, answering is hardly worth the effort. The interest shown will amplify or throttle the thinking of the speaker. This idea is so important, I'm going to repeat it. *Your level of interest determines how well the other person can think.*

So how can we tell when someone is curious? Perhaps it's in their tone. They might speak more slowly with greater emphasis. They might show it in their face, their body language. Perhaps they lean in. We'll talk more about body language later.

When an active listener asks a question, they ask it like the answer matters to them. Do that.

Okay, now we can move on to the L.

Listen to the response

When we're actively listening, we're really paying attention. We're focused on the speaker, what they're saying with words, what they're saying with their bodies and how they're doing it.

Optimal listening is an act of generosity. It's not rushed. It's patient. It's highly attentive. When the speaker experiences your listening in this way, they'll think more deeply and creatively. They've got time to think.

Great listening pays attention to the content – what's being said. You might need to jot down some notes if there's a lot of detail. Don't try to keep track in your head – you have finite cognitive energy too.

Great listening pays attention to how things are being said. Occasionally people will speak in bold or italics.

They emphasise certain words or ideas. Notice when this happens. They're telling you something important.

Great listening is non-judgemental. The listener doesn't feel they are being judged or evaluated while they're talking. It's safe to speak. You're an ally. Speakers will look to check how what they're saying is landing for you. They're looking for clues that you may be critical. Don't give them any.

Great listening is interested. You care about what's being said. The speaker has the experience that you care. This catalyses thinking. How do you know if someone cares about what you say? What are the clues? Maybe you can tell from their expression, their encouraging sounds or from their rapt attention. Interested listeners are curious listeners.

Pause before responding

Being quiet is hard for many of us. Most conversations are like games of ping pong. The conversational ball is whacked over the net the instant it arrives. The ball never pauses in mid-air.

When we're actively listening, we'll occasionally pause when the speaker stops talking. Just for a moment. We open up a small space between voices. It could be for a tenth of a second. Or a half second. Advanced listeners are comfortable being quieter for much longer.

This has several positive consequences:

- It gives you a moment to consider what you're going to say next, taking into consideration the last thing you heard.

- It shows the speaker that you're considering what they've just said (you haven't just been waiting for them to shut up).

- It prevents the speaker from feeling rushed.

- It prevents you from derailing the speaker's thinking. Maybe they haven't finished.

- Maybe they have finished. But the gift of silence allows them to think further and articulate any new ideas that bubble up in the space.

The ability to be momentarily silent is a conversational superpower few possess. Build it.

Occasionally students tell me they worry the speaker will think their micro-moment of silence will be interpreted as meaning they've zoned out. You can remedy this by nodding slowly while you're suffering the agony of not speaking for a second. If you have a flamboyant moustache, you might twiddle the ends thoughtfully. Do what you must to indicate to the speaker that you're still alive, awake and taking their words seriously. You'll cope, with or without facial hair … honest.

Acknowledging what we heard

Great listeners acknowledge *that* they're hearing, and *what* they're hearing.

You've had that experience of talking on the phone and you don't hear anything for a bit. 'Hello, hello … are you still there?' When we're actively listening, on the phone or in person, we need to continually reassure the speaker that we're still there. Still present and paying attention.

You might do this with a nod, an 'mmm', an 'I see' or 'right … '. These are known as 'minimal encouragers'. They tell the speaker that you're paying attention, and they should continue.

After the speaker has stopped speaking and you've paused (did you remember to pause?), the active listener acknowledges *what* they've just heard. They summarise the gist of what's been said.

This is sometimes called 'paraphrasing'. Strictly speaking, paraphrasing is putting something into your own words. Your own words are wonderful, really, but the speaker's own words are more meaningful to the speaker. Try to use a few of the speaker's own words if you can.

You might acknowledge what you've just heard in a single word or by mirroring the last few words. Acknowledging what you've just heard is another superpower. When listeners do this:

· **Speakers feel heard.** You must have really been paying attention. They sense your interest.

- **It develops empathy and rapport.** Speakers feel validated. Understood. You get them.

- **Speakers get perspective on their own thinking.** When we are hearing our own words come back to us, we have a chance to consider them. *Was that what I really meant?* We get an opportunity to clarify and revise our initial thinking.

The experience of feeling validated is especially empowering. This doesn't mean you necessarily agree with what's been said, but you're confirming that you got the message. You see where they're coming from. As a result, speakers feel understood, and they may understand themselves a little more too. They are more likely to lower their defences, accept uncomfortable truths and change their minds.

Check your understanding

After acknowledging what's been said, the active listener checks they've understood correctly. It could be as brief as, 'Have I got that right?'

Your conversation is improved by whatever answer you get.

Let's say the speaker says no, that's not it at all. Well, you've given them an opportunity to correct you. You've just demonstrated you care enough to want to understand correctly. They'll feel heard. It will build rapport. And you've learnt something.

Let's say the speaker says yes, that's it! You've just demonstrated you care enough to want to understand correctly. They'll feel heard. It will build rapport. And you've learnt something.

This check does something else too. Something that may be even more important. It gives the speaker another opportunity to consider their own thinking with a bit of distance. They'll get perspective. Often speakers will correct, clarify and continue their own thinking and speaking after you've checked your understanding.

If they don't keep speaking, then you could …

Ask another question

The question you'll ask is probably going to be a follow-up question. It's relevant to what's just been discussed. Maybe you're looking for some clarification or development of an idea.

As you're aware, when we read text online, some of it is hyperlinked. It's underlined or in bold, and when you click it you're taken to another page. When people speak, it's as if some of the words they say are hyperlinked. If you click on them by asking a question, they'll share a lot more information.

Maybe someone says:

'I'd like to get **better** at presentations.'

'The finance department is being **difficult**.'

'The client is **daunted**.'

It's tempting to assume we know exactly what they mean. Maybe we do. But it's better to clarify what the speaker means by clicking on the word. You might say:

'Better?'

'Difficult?'

'Daunted?'

If necessary, bolt on 'tell me more', or 'say more about that', or the ever flexible 'go on'.

A terrific general follow-up question is the AWE question[6]: *And What Else?* Your initial question has been answered. Now you ask, 'And what else?' You run through the ALPACA model again and once more ask, 'And what else?' You might do this several times before finishing with an, 'Anything else?'

As with all questions, *how* you ask the AWE question is crucial. Ask it like you expect there is something else and you're keen to hear what it is. I've lost count of the number of times my coachees have come up with new insights after being asked the AWE question. And I'm good at counting!

An empowering question is one the individual hasn't yet asked themselves. Often people haven't asked themselves 'and what else'? They came up with their initial thoughts

---

6   Credit to Michael Bungay Stanier for this question, which you'll find in his excellent book, *The Coaching Habit*. Not only a great read, this book is also beautifully presented. I'd like to acknowledge the influence that *The Coaching Habit* has had on the presentation of *The Coach-like Leader*.

and stopped there. They stopped because thinking new thoughts is tiring. Curiously, we're all willing to put in more effort in the presence of other people. It's why people go to exercise classes. Of course, they could go to the gym and always train alone. But we're generally willing to go further and try harder for longer when we're with other people.

The coach-like leader helps others think further and try harder for longer. The AWE question helps here. Thinking for longer and harder can be effortful.

A word about effort. Thinking routine familiar thoughts is effortless, thinking new thoughts is effortful. A sign of a great coaching conversation is that the coachee is a bit tired afterwards. Good! It means they've been exercising their neurons. You wanted to challenge them, after all. You did it.

* * *

The ALPACA framework is just a guide. In real life you'll skip bits. You might change the order. You might choose to break the 'rules' occasionally and interrupt the speaker (gasp!), or tell them something you've been thinking. Improvise. Do what works. What works won't always be what's easiest. Easy isn't the objective. The point is to communicate in a way that helps someone else think, learn, plan and take action. Experiment and discover for yourself.

6: The GROW Model

"The best way to **predict the future** is to create it."

Peter Drucker

f you wanted to build a house, you'd need to assemble the appropriate building blocks with the relevant skills in the optimal order. No point putting the roof on first, right?

We're not building houses, but we are constructing conversations. We've already discussed several skills and building blocks for coaching conversations such as asking questions, being solution-focused, giving others autonomy and the responsibility to think, plan and act.

So, what sequence should we follow when assembling our conversational building blocks? The best-known coaching model is (ta da!) GROW. There are plenty of others, but between you and me, they're harder to remember and all broadly do the same thing.

By itself, GROW is not coaching. Many rushed professionals have whipped through an introductory course to the GROW model and have been misled into thinking they can now coach. To be successfully applied, GROW must be used flexibly and skilfully. All the conditions of coaching must be met. Poorly trained leaders inevitably end up using this model clinically and rigidly. Team members fail to engage as expected and the uncoach-like leaders blame the tool. The truth is that they didn't work skilfully with the model.

The good news is you only need elementary coaching skills to discover that this simple model is surprisingly powerful. It will guide your conversations in a productive direction. Here are the four stages and some examples of the kinds of questions you might ask in each stage.

GROW

COACHING IN 4 STEPS

REALITY
WHERE ARE YOU NOW?

WILL
WHAT WILL YOU DO?

GOAL
WHAT DO YOU WANT?

OPTIONS
WHAT COULD YOU DO?

"**Frameworks provide the scaffolding for success**, guiding us through the intricate architecture of problem-solving."

Anonymous

GOAL

What do you want?

Remember what leadership guru Stephen Covey told us in *The Seven Habits of Highly Effective People* – **begin with the end in mind.** According to Stephen, effective leaders know where they're going before they set off. In coaching we help others decide up front what a great outcome would look like in relation to the topic at hand.

So, what is the topic and what would you like to have happen? What would success look like? What positive impacts would that have? Why does that matter?

Don't rush this stage. The success of the rest of the model depends upon identifying a compelling goal and clarifying the why. This releases motivational juices to fuel courageous and creative thinking.

Don't expect the one true final objective to be instantly identified and set in stone. Rather expect goals to evolve as you ask clarifying questions, such as:

- What's on your mind?
- What would you like to have happen?
- What would you like to accomplish?
- What result are you trying to achieve?
- What do you really want?
- What would be the ideal outcome?
- What would you like to be different?
- Why does this really matter?
- What are the positive outcomes from achieving this goal?
- What's most important about achieving this?
- What are the implications of doing nothing?
- If you achieved this, what would it be like?
- What does success look like?

REALITY

Where are you now?

This stage is an exploration of the coachee's current situation. The leader helps the team member gain a clear understanding of their present reality – what's happening now, what are the challenges, what resources are available, what's been tried and with what results?

This stage also involves examining the gaps between the coachee's current reality and their desired outcomes, fostering awareness of areas that require improvement or change. It's the gap between the present and an improved future that motivates action.

When challenged with daunting problems, people sometimes overlook what's working well. The coach-like leader will also inquire about successes and exceptions to any presenting problems. When hasn't the problem shown up? What may have contributed to that positive result? Ask:

- What's happening now/what's the situation now?
- What's the real challenge here for you?
- What have you already tried?
- Where are you now in relation to your goal?
- On a scale of 1 to 10, where are you now?
- What progress have you made so far?
- What's working well at the moment?
- What is being asked of you?
- What obstacles are in the way of achieving your goal?

OPTIONS

What could you do?

The options stage is where the coachee and coach collaboratively brainstorm and evaluate potential strategies and solutions to address the challenges and goals. What are actionable options for moving forward?

The coach-like leader facilitates this process by encouraging the coachee to think creatively and consider a wide range of possibilities. Together, they explore the pros and cons of each option, considering factors such as feasibility, impact and alignment with the team member's values and objectives.

Effective coach-like leaders catalyse the creativity of others through demonstrating their belief and trust that others do in fact have more options. Ask:

- What are some of your options?
- What else?
- And what else?
- What have others done in this situation?
- Who else may be able to help?
- What's the hardest/most challenging part of that for you?
- What advice would you give to a friend about that?
- What would be the consequence of doing that?
- What could you do differently?
- If anything was possible, what would you do?
- What's the best thing about that option?
- What's the worst thing about that option?

WILL

What will you do?

In the will stage, the coachee solidifies their commitment to take specific actions and follow through on the decisions made during the previous stages. What specifically will they do and when will they do it?

This stage is all about translating plans into action and overcoming potential obstacles or resistance.

The coach helps the coachee establish a timeline and action steps, breaking down larger objectives into smaller, manageable tasks. They also explore potential barriers and challenges that may arise, discussing strategies to mitigate these obstacles.

The coach plays a supportive role, holding the coachee accountable for their commitments and helping them stay motivated and focused. Ask:

- What's the first step?
- How will you do it?
- When will you take this first step?
- What's the cost of you not taking action?
- What do you need from others to help you do this?
- What resources do you need?
- What obstacles may get in the way of success?
- What can you do to handle those obstacles?
- Is there anything missing?

Some final thoughts about the GROW model. In real conversations you'll probably never visit each stage just once in the order given. You'll bounce about a bit. So, treat it as a suggested framework. However, always do the following:

· Get clear about the goal early in the conversation.

· Visit each stage at least once.

· Finish with an explicit commitment to the next step.

So, rather than having a GROW conversation, you'll probably have more of a GRGORGOGOW conversation. Just make sure you begin with G and finish with W. Otherwise you're not coaching.

The future belongs to those who act. **Seize the present, shape tomorrow.**

7: Body Talk

"**Your body communicates to the world**, whether you want it to or not."

Olivia Fox Cabane

O ur ancestors started walking upright on a Thursday five million years ago. Thereabouts. We couldn't talk yet but we got along with meaning-ful gestures, postures, expressions and sounds. We collaborated through hunting, foraging, sharing and defending – all done wordlessly. Two-and-a-half million years ago we started creating tools such as hammers and blades, and training each other to make and use them. Teamwork without talking.

Paleoanthropologists tell us humans started speaking relatively recently, about 70,000 years ago. Apparently, that's when we evolved the throat structures and the brains required. This means that for 98.6% of the time since we've been upright, we've worked together without saying a word. Isn't that amazing? Some of us might even say they were the good old days!

When speaking finally showed up, it didn't replace body language – it supplemented it. We are still very sensitive to what others are telling us without words. It's often said that body language trumps spoken language, that actions speak louder than words. When someone's body language isn't quite aligned with what they're saying, our phoniness detection systems are activated. The speaker loses credibility and we're guarded and defensive. Not helpful in coaching.

When you're having any kind of conversation, coaching or otherwise, you're always communicating with your body and sometimes with words. Effective coach-like leaders are mindful of both and seek to align them.

We all care, at least a little, what others think of us. This doesn't make you needy, it makes you mindful. Considerate of the impact you're having. Socially intelligent. We're especially interested in what our leaders think of us. Their opinions matter even more. As a result, when you're coaching a report, they're probably asking themselves various questions, without even realising it:

- Is this person interested in what I have to say?
- Are they glad to be with me?
- Do I matter to them?
- Do they believe in my capability?
- Do they value me, my role, my contributions and my potential?

Effective coach-like leaders ensure their body language is experienced by others as interested, appreciative, trusting, respectful and supportive. This combination of experiences is especially empowering.

So, what kind of body postures, gestures and other non-verbal communication might be helpful and what do

we want to avoid? It all depends on the culture and con-
text. Some things are deeply respectful in one culture and
unspeakably rude in another. In some cultures, non-verbals
should be subtle, in others flamboyant. So we must drive to
the conditions.

Here are some ideas to get you going.

People who are	Often do this	And not this
pleased to see you	smile	frown
interested	lean forward	slump
curious	widen their eyes	freeze their expressions
open to your thinking	open their posture	cross their arms and legs
attentive	give you eye contact	check their phone
understanding	nod	shake their head
accepting	nod	roll their eyes
encouraging	make supportive sounds	are silent
present	watch you	watch the clock or check email
respectful	look across at you	look down at you

Elevate your online conversations

Conversations are increasingly held online. Meetings, presentations and check-ins that would previously have been conducted face to face are now often done virtually. You can expect many of your coaching conversations will be held online.

There are many ways you can improve your online conversations. Here are five things to consider.

ELEVATE YOUR ONLINE CONVERSATIONS

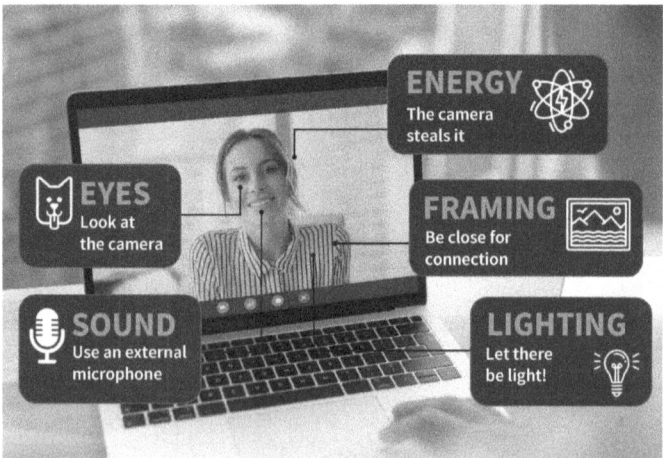

1. Eyes

Did you know that the world's most popular pet is the dog? There are many reasons for this, including goofy smiles, excited tail wagging and unconditional devotion. But there's one other feature that dogs excel at that has put them in the #1 spot for popular pets: they're great at making and holding eye contact. This connects us in a way other pets can only dream of.

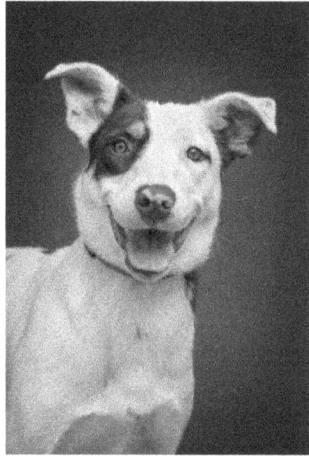

When most people are speaking online, they generally don't quite make eye contact. They're looking at the video of the person they're speaking to, typically below the webcam and sometimes on a different monitor. When someone isn't making eye contact, we notice. Of course, we make allowances for this – we understand what's going on. Trying to make eye contact on screen is not the same as face to face. But people who can establish eye contact, even when they're online, are experienced differently. As the viewer you feel more connected. There's greater rapport. This is of course important for coaching.

One way to achieve eye contact online is for the speaker to look at the webcam. Not always, but for about 70% of the time. That way you can still keep an eye on how the other person is responding. It can feel a little odd at first but the impact on the person you're addressing is powerful.

An alternative is to position the image of the person you're speaking to as close to the webcam as possible, perhaps shrinking it in the process. I suggest doing this and speaking to the webcam. That way you can move between the two with minimal eye movements.

2. Sound

When coaching, it's especially important that you're easy to understand. Your voice should be crystal clear. That way there's no effort required to interpret what you've just said. The clearer your voice, the better the connection. You'll feel closer. It builds rapport. You may have had this experience occasionally when calling someone overseas with your smartphone. These apps are so good it can feel like that person on the other side of the planet is in the same room as you. That's the experience we're aiming for.

Laptop microphones are generally poor quality. Not only that, but your mouth is probably a couple of feet away. Microphones are designed to work best when your mouth is a few inches away.

The solution is to use an external microphone. Headsets are excellent, and if you're going to spend many hours online, consider investing in a high-quality USB microphone. I consider doing this one of the best tech purchases I've ever made.

3. Lighting

We trust people we can see. We like to see the expressions and eyes of the people we're talking to. Don't be a shady silhouette with a bright light behind you. That's appropriate for lethal agent James Bond at the start of his movies but not for the psychologically safe coach-like leader.

Webcams are thirsty for light. They operate at their highest resolution when the subject is bathed in light. To be clear and credible, ensure you're well lit. Use a desk lamp, an inexpensive ring-light or free sunshine from the front – let there be light.

4. Framing

Take a look at the woman in the image earlier in this chapter. She's perfectly positioned for online work. She's occupying a lot of the frame and as a result the viewer will feel close to her. This is important for connection in coaching. It's hard to feel connected to someone who's small and in the background, or who has part of their head cut off.

It's also a good idea to have the webcam at eye level so the viewer feels like they're at the same height as you. If you just plonk your laptop on a desk, odds are that the viewer can see your ceiling. They have the impression of looking up at you. This is good if you want to intimidate someone or patronise them. It's inappropriate when we're having a collaborative conversation. Level the camera.

5. Energy

It's an odd thing but cameras steal energy if you let them. People find themselves a little more muted and a little less expressive when they're in front of a webcam. You may need to dial up the energy in your responses when you're on camera. Make your gestures and expressions a little more conspicuous. Show a little more emotion.

Start strong

Whether you're online or in person, how you begin is pivotal. Those first few moments are disproportionately important. They set the tone for the entire conversation. So, demonstrate that you're glad to see your team member; this is something you've been looking forward to, it's a pleasure. If you're perceived as slightly distracted, impatient or displeased at the very start, it's unlikely you'll have a productive interaction.

The initial moments of an encounter are like the opening lines of a book. **Craft them with care**; they decide whether someone continues reading your story.

8: Motivation Matters

"There are only two ways to **influence human behavior**: you can manipulate it, or you can inspire it."

Simon Sinek

We all do much better work when we're feeling energised, engaged and motivated. Motivation helps us think. Take action. Learn. It gets us up and going. It activates our brains and bodies.

Some tasks are inherently motivating for teams. They're fun, interesting and enjoyable. Maybe there's a bonus dangling, an opportunity to travel or build skills. Leaders will then have no need to develop further motivation. Other tasks are, well, considerably less appealing. But they still need to be done.

Coach-like leaders are skilled at helping others tap into and amplify their own motivations. This can help people work on what matters most.

Maximising motivation

Here are five ways to maximise motivation in team members who aren't feeling it. These principles are effective only when applied in combination with the conditions for coaching we discussed in chapter 2 (mutual respect, positive expectations and psychological safety).

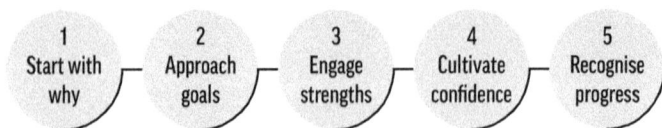

1 Start with why	2 Approach goals	3 Engage strengths	4 Cultivate confidence	5 Recognise progress

1. Start with why

People are generally more motivated to do things for their own reasons, not for ours. If you need to boost a team member's motivation for a task or project, help them find a way to make it personally appealing. What's *their* why? What does this person care about, what matters to them, what do they value?

Although people obviously value external rewards such as being paid and promoted, we're also profoundly impacted by internal rewards. By our personal values.

Personal values are freely chosen ways of showing up in life and work. When our actions are values-aligned, activities feel worthwhile. We're being the kind of people we aspire to be. We can be justifiably proud of our efforts. Values-aligned work is inherently rewarding and motivating.

When our work is out of step with our personal values, our heart won't be in it. It's not who we are. It's inauthentic.

Coaches can help build motivation in others by exploring their personal and professional ambitions. What kind of person do they aspire to be? What qualities do they choose to practise and develop? What would make them proud?

Coach-like leaders know their people and understand what matters most to them. Team members reveal their personal values through what they talk about and how they talk about it. They'll be energised and animated when discussing values-aligned actions, and annoyed or angry when they discuss events at work or in the news that violate personal values. Indirectly, people are always telling you what matters to them. Values can also be identified with online assessments.[7]

The following image provides some examples of personal values.

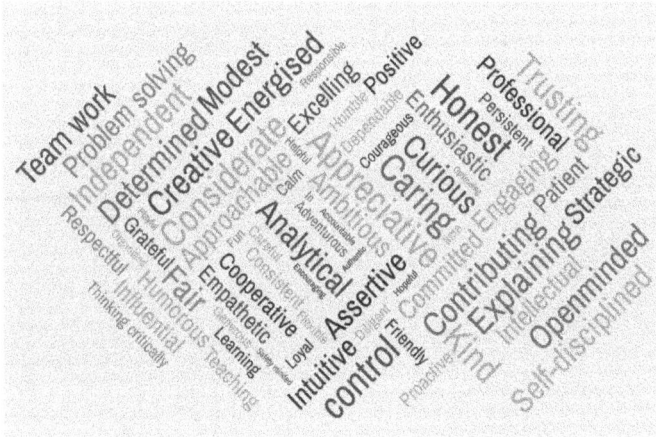

When team member motivation needs a boost, explore ways to make tasks more values-aligned. *Their* why will always energise engagement to a greater extent than *your* why.

---

7   For example, https://personalvalu.es.

2. Approach goals

When all's said and done, people are motivated by just two things: to move towards rewards and away from threats. They both ignite action, but in different ways and with different consequences. Effective coach-like leaders are mindful of the differences.

MOTIVATION TO AVOID THREAT

When we're driven primarily by threat avoidance, we're doing something because we feel we have to, not because we want to. We're being coerced. There's no real autonomy. Experiences we might want to avoid at work include:

· the loss of a bonus
· displeasing our manager
· letting colleagues down
· doing a poor job
· missing out on a promotion.

Like salt, a sprinkling of fear can be a good thing. Some clear downsides to inaction will help us to get going. But when overused, it spoils the taste of work.

It's draining to be operating in a perpetual state of threat. Excessive worry debilitates. It undermines our ability to focus, innovate and collaborate. In a state of worry we think more about *me* and less about *we*.

When we're driven mostly by fear and we succeed in achieving our goals, the end result is brief relief. Phew!

But the satisfaction doesn't last. Avoidance goals are a kind of junk food for mental health. They can never promote wellbeing or fuel a high-performance career.

Fear does have its place as a motivator for occasional use for short-term goals, but it's an exhausting way to live over the longer term. It's just not sustainable.

MOTIVATION TO APPROACH REWARDS

When we're driven primarily by rewards, we're approaching something attractive to us. Experiences we might want more of at work include:

- participation in an interesting project
- an appealing challenge
- an opportunity to learn new skills
- a chance to travel
- a values-aligned activity
- a meaningful outcome for others (colleagues or the community)
- a meaningful outcome for ourselves (status, bonus, promotion).

We're taking action because we choose to.

It's energising to be operating in a state of approach. It fuels creative thinking; we explore and discover possibilities. We're bolder. We learn more effectively. We're engaged and willing.

When we succeed in achieving our goals, the end result is satisfaction and pride. Plus, better working relationships, greater knowledge and experiences.

Approach motivation can be used for short-term and long-term goals. It's sustainable.

Coach-like leaders help team members define approach goals.

3. Engage strengths

Everyone likes to feel as though they know what they're doing. No one likes to feel in over their heads. You may recall that competence is one of the three needs everyone shares (the others being autonomy and relatedness).

We also like to learn stuff. There's a joy in discovering how to do something new or better. Each time we become a bit more competent, it feels good. Tasks are more motivating when we see them as opportunities to use our strengths and to develop.

When coaching someone to boost their motivation, frame the task as an opportunity to engage existing skills and strengths. You can identify strengths through observation or by doing an online strengths assessment.

There are two especially popular strengths assessments: Cappfinity Strengths Profile[8] and Gallup CliftonStrengths.[9]

---

8   www.strengthsprofile.com.
9   www.gallup.com/cliftonstrengths.

The following image provides some examples of personal strengths.

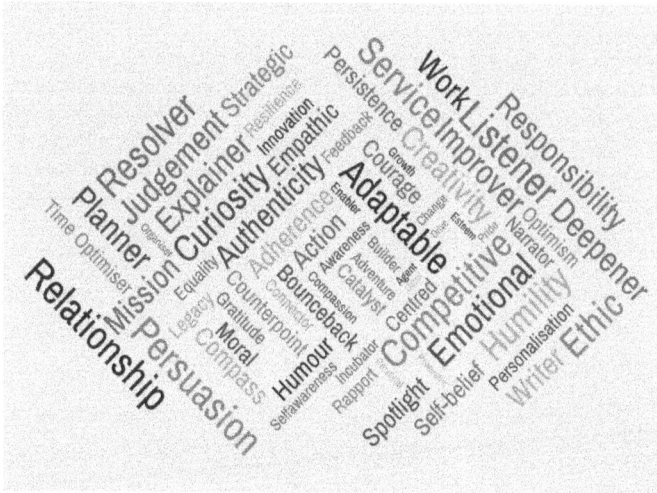

Effective coach-like leaders know their team members' strengths, name them when they're expressed and help others to own them. It's who they are at their best.

4. Cultivate confidence

People are motivated at work when they have an appealing goal and believe they have what it takes to achieve it, in the time available. Resources are external and internal. Necessary external resources include team support, technology, time, finances and leadership endorsement.

A critical internal resource in igniting motivation for action is confidence. Trusting you can do it. Believing you can:

- initiate action
- sustain action
- build alliances
- cope with setbacks
- learn from setbacks
- apply necessary skills
- address skill gaps
- manage physical and emotional energy.

Enduring confidence isn't something created through positive affirmations. It's built through personal experiences of success and the belief others have in us. Sometimes the opinions of others matter more than our own.

Effective coach-like leaders believe in the capabilities and potential of their team members, and they express this. When their people have a win they celebrate it and help them absorb a deserved sense of competency. Mastery experiences like this have been shown to be the most powerful way to boost confidence. Help your people upgrade their identity by recognising success when it happens.

A sense of confidence is also boosted by observing others doing what we want to do. Seeing something done by another person makes a task instantly more doable.

A coach might demonstrate a skill to a team member to build their belief that it can indeed be done.

Self-efficacy is also enhanced by coaching people to break down large goals into smaller, more achievable goals. This is a useful strategy whenever a task or project is daunting: chunk it down into bite-sized pieces.

5. Recognise progress

If you've ever played a computer game, you'll know they often include levels. You start on one level and you work your way up. Game designers understand that there's something weirdly compelling about the experience of making progress. I confess I've got a game on my phone called Homescapes that I find strangely addictive. Don't install it – it's a complete waste of time. It doesn't tap into my strengths, provide value or enable me to achieve anything worthwhile in my personal or professional life. However, it makes skillful use of the progress principle. You really feel like you're getting somewhere, and that it matters!

The Progress Principle, by Teresa Amabile and Steven Kramer, explores the idea that progress, even small and incremental, is a key driver of motivation and happiness in the workplace. They argue that when individuals experience progress in their work, it has a positive impact on their motivation, creativity and overall wellbeing. Extensive research apparently finds that the experience of daily progress, regardless of its size, can significantly influence an individual's sense of accomplishment and job satisfaction. They emphasise the importance of recognising and supporting progress in the workplace to foster a more motivated and engaged workforce.

Comedian Jerry Seinfeld attributes much of his success to the principle of tracking progress. From the very beginning of his career, he made a commitment to write at least one new joke every day. Each time he did so, he put a cross on his calendar. At a glance he can see how much progress he's made and it's motivating. More than that, he can't abide the thought of breaking his multi-year joke-writing streak.

Coach-like leaders recognise, track and celebrate the progress of team members and encourage them to do the same for themselves.

"The best way to motivate people, day in and day out, **is by facilitating progress** – even small wins."

Teresa Amabile

9: Challenges to Coaching

"The obstacle is **the way**."

Emperor Marcus Aurelius

Once you fully embrace the fact that effective coaching is an essential part of building a high-performing and motivated team, what could possibly get in your way?

Here are some common obstacles. Expect them. Plan for them.

⧖ TIME CONSTRAINTS

You've got competing responsibilities and a busy schedule. Finding time to dedicate to coaching can be difficult. Perhaps some of your team members live and work in different time zones, further complicating scheduling coaching conversations. Coaching is most effective when it's consistent, and unpredictable workloads and time-sensitive tasks often disrupt the best laid plans. Finding the time to consistently provide personalised attention to each employee can be difficult.

POTENTIAL SOLUTIONS

- **Quick coaching:** you don't always need a lot of time. Make the most of brief, informal interactions.
- **Prioritise coaching:** allocate dedicated time slots and protect them as you would any other important task.
- **Schedule regularly:** ensure coaching is a consistent part of your routine.
- **Delegate:** delegate tasks and responsibilities to team members, to free up your time for coaching conversations.
- **Use technology:** team members don't need to be onsite. Use video calls where possible to ease scheduling constraints.

RESISTANT EMPLOYEES

You already know how many people it takes to tango. Same for coaching. Great coaching conversations depend on both participants, well, participating. The employee must be ready and willing to cooperate in this conversational dance.

A number of things can fuel resistance. Perhaps you've already established a working relationship with someone and it was a primarily directive one. They're accustomed to you giving instructions and answers. If you suddenly change your style of managing without notice, expect resistance.

I'd love to tell you that *everyone* wants to be coached, but that would be a fib. Some folks aren't interested in collaborating in thinking and planning. They just want instructions.

It is my experience though that all high-potential employees jump at the chance to engage in coaching.

POTENTIAL SOLUTIONS

- **Evaluate coachability:** you may work in an environment in which some of your team members are not going to be coachable. In some organisations you'll need to be selective about who you coach and who you don't. Focus your coaching efforts on those who will engage and benefit.

- **Give them notice:** before coaching someone for the first time, let them know your intentions. You might say that to help them develop their skills and capability you would like to have a different kind of conversation occasionally, one in which you'll be asking more questions and encouraging them to participate in decision making. And you're doing this because you can see they've got a lot of potential. Would that be okay?

THE ADVICE MONSTER

This isn't going away. The urge to tell others what you think they should do will always be there, especially if you're skilled in doing what your people are doing. I've coached senior leadership for over 10 years – I still have the urge to chip in with suggestions. Sometimes, the best coach-like leaders are those with less technical skill than their people – that way they're unable to contaminate the team's thinking with their brilliant suggestions. They don't have any. Instead, they catalyse their team's thinking with empowering questions.

The advice monster is cunning, and will attempt to seduce you into giving advice disguised as questions, so you think you're coaching:

- 'Have you thought about … ?'
- 'Why don't you … ?'
- 'What about … ?'

Such questions are a kind of Trojan horse. Keep them stabled.

POTENTIAL SOLUTION

- **Notice → Pause → Choose:** a great way to manage unhelpful urges of all types is to get better at noticing them as they arise. Urges have a telltale feeling in the body – your throat might tighten as you sense an urgency to speak. **Notice** how your advice monster shows up. Recognise it as it shuffles forward. Then **pause** – this is the really skillful part. Pausing in the presence of an insistent advice monster is an act of emotional intelligence. This act of defiant restraint is something we can all get better at with practice.

And then **choose**. Will you delay giving advice a little longer? Or is it appropriate to share your thinking now?

PSYCHOLOGICAL SAFETY

You'll recall the experience of psychological safety enables people to:

· disagree
· ask for help
· admit mistakes
· challenge groupthink
· voice their thoughts.

To be effectively coached, people need to speak without fear of being judged, criticised or assessed. Such fears throttle the ability to brainstorm, to explore possibilities, to discover insights only accessible through thinking out loud with a trusted thought partner.

POTENTIAL SOLUTIONS

· **Get to know each other:** we trust those we're comfortable with, and we're comfortable with people we know. Learn more about your people, and let them know more about you.

· **Build trust:** we earn trust through demonstrations of being trustworthy. Doing what we said we would, honouring confidential disclosures, admitting our mistakes, giving credit where it's due, saying when we don't know the answer and asking for help ourselves. This can take time.

· **Be non-judgemental:** when your team boldly share challenges, concerns and difficulties, respond with support and be non-judgemental. When people learn they really can tell you anything and you'll be there for them, they'll increasingly think more effectively in your presence.

· **Walk the talk:** treat everyone fairly so all feel psychological safety. People are watching and people talk. If just one person feels embarrassed, humiliated or belittled, others will find out and be on guard.

· **Be real:** we feel safe with consistently authentic people.

SKILLS GAP

Coaching skills take time to develop and embed. Skills such as active listening, solution-focused conversations, asking empowering questions, withholding advice and really being present are skills that we develop through practice. Attending a coaching skills training course gives you a great springboard. But it's what you do next that will develop your coaching capability.

POTENTIAL SOLUTIONS

· **Peer coaching:** practise coaching conversations with someone else who has done this training. Give each other feedback. Let each other know what you found helpful and what was less helpful.

· **Be professionally coached:** you'll discover firsthand what promotes your thinking, and what derails it. It's a terrific way to improve your coaching. I've been coached by others throughout my career – yes, it helps me with my own ambitions, but I'm also using the experience to improve my coaching.

· **Practise coaching skills separately:** coaching comprises multiple skills. You can practise them individually. You might set an intention at the start of the day to practise one throughout the day. It could be active listening, or a single component of active listening.

· **Practise coaching skills combined:** even having short coaching check-ins will give you an opportunity to practise a combination of coaching skills.

Off to Great Places!

"You're off to Great Places! **Today is your day!** Your mountain is waiting, so get on your way!"

Dr Seuss

Congratulations are in order. Well done you on investing in your capability development. Your coaching skills will change lives – yours and the people you live and work with. A coach-like leader is a more empowering human being. That means you're even more awesome than you were before, and that's saying something!

Your coaching skills will continue to grow as you practise them. I encourage you to both coach and be coached, by colleagues, an internal workplace coach or an external one. Experiencing coaching firsthand will accelerate your proficiency. You'll notice what catalyses your thinking and what suppresses it. I attended my first coaching training over 14 years ago, and I've both coached and been coached continually since then. Strongly recommended.

I wish you well in your coaching skills journey to your own Great Places. If you have any queries about anything in this book, feel free to send me an email. I'd also love to hear about the positive impact applying these skills has had on your leadership. Do let me know.

Eric Winters hello@ericwinters.com.au

Acknowledgements

I'm doomed. There's no way of doing this section justice. I've learned from so very many about how to coach, and how to teach. Names will be missed. Offense will be taken. So be it.

Instead of writing one of those interminable lists of names usually seen in acknowledgements, I'll just call out two special people and one extraordinary group. As usual, I'll keep it brief.

Special person 1: John Franklin, the Director of Coaching and Positive Psychology at Macquarie University. John was my first coaching teacher. His wonderful style of teaching initiated a fascination in the topic. He was awesome. John would have appeared in this section solely for his teaching but he did something else that changed my life. It was John who directed me to seek further training from:

Special person 2: Tony Grant, the Director of the Coaching Psychology Unit at the University of Sydney. Not only a global thought leader and pioneer in the field of coaching psychology, Tony was also a very funny guy. I do like funny. Tony's no longer with us but his impact on evidence-based coaching reverberates around the planet. Not only did Tony teach me coaching, he taught me how to teach in a way that was engaging, humorous and human. Tony equipped me to share what I'd learned with:

Extraordinary group 1: My students. As sci-fi author Robert Heinlein said, "when one teaches, two learn". I've taught over a thousand coaching workshop participants, both private and public sector leaders, and professional coaches, in person and online, and have learned how to be a better teacher in every workshop. Thank you all. I might wrap up by mentioning I've been especially inspired by Australian Public Service leaders in government agencies. Those who serve deserve all our thanks. I've spent many enjoyable hours running workshops for agencies such as The Department of Defence, The Department of Veterans Affairs and the Department of Foreign Affairs and Trade, who, I want to acknowledge, also have the very best canteen.

About Eric

I live in Sydney with my partner Rachel and Oliver, the one-eyed rescue cat. I spend my work life facilitating leadership development workshops and delivering keynotes on coaching, courage and emotional intelligence.

I'm also the author of *Swipe Right on Your Best Self: Simple steps to a bolder life with fewer regrets.*

That's Oliver in the middle.

Feel free to connect on LinkedIn: www.linkedin.com/in/coachlikeleader.

.